Problems With Modern Monetary Theory: A Comment on Stephanie Kelton's "The Deficit Myth"

Problems With Modern Monetary Theory: A Comment on Stephanie Kelton's "The Deficit Myth"

Robert Wenzel

Gallatin House

Copyright 2020 Gallatin House LLC

All Rights Reserved. Printed in the United States of America. No part of this book may be used or reproduced in any manner whatsoever without written permission, except in the case of brief quotations embodied in critical articles and reviews. For information content books@gallatinhouse.com

FIRST EDITION August 2020

ISBN 978-1-71664-638-6

Library of Congress Cataloging-in-Publication Data

Wenzel, Robert

Subject headings:
Modern monetary theory.
United States-Deficit spending.
United States-Economic policy.
United States-Government Spending Policy
Job guarantee.

Cover Design by Thomas Rossini

Published by Gallatin House LLC

TABLE OF CONTENTS

INTRODUCTION	10
CHAPTER 1: JUST PRINT MONEY, MONEY, MONEY AND MORE MONEY	14
CHAPTER 2: TAXES AND THE DEVELOPMENT OF MONEY	16
CHAPTER 3: PRICE INFLATION	22
CHAPTER 4: HATING THE RICH	30
CHAPTER 5: ANTI-TRADE	36
CHAPTER 6: DEFICITS DON'T MATTER	42
CONCLUSION	48

INTRODUCTION

Modern Monetary Theory (MMT) is hot with the greater chattering class. It is the only reason I am writing this extended comment. The theory needs to be deconstructed, to be blown up, before it is taken seriously beyond the chattering class and by more policymakers.

There is nothing new at the core of MMT and the old it is promoting in a fancy new dress is bad economics.

MMT has been gaining in popularity in the financial and general media, in some parts of academia, and with some of the more radical leftist members of the United States Congress.

In her new book, *The Deficit Myth: Modern Monetary Theory and the Birth of the People's Economy,* Stephanie Kelton specifically acknowledges the help given to her by Joe Wiesenthal, executive editor of news for Bloomberg Digital, Neil Cavuto, a Fox Business host, Fareed Zakaria, host of CNN's Fareed Zakaria GPS.

Farhad Manjoo at *The New York Times* writes:

> Stephanie Kelton convincingly overturns the conventional wisdom that federal budget deficits are somehow bad for the nation. ...Kelton argues that our government's inability to provide for citizens isn't due

to a lack for money; instead, our leaders lack political will.[1]

Kelton also singled out for acknowledgment the Democratic-socialist congresswoman Alexandria Ocasio-Cortez.

Senator Bernie Sanders, a socialist, was responsible for getting Kelton the position of Chief Economist for the Democratic minority staff on the US Senate's budget committee. She held that position in 2015 and early 2016, and left to become an economic advisor to the Sanders 2016 presidential campaign. Her book has appeared on *The New York Times* best seller list.

It is not surprising that Kelton finds strong support from the left to the extreme left. Her proposals call for extreme central planning and her monetary theory supports aggressive government spending. According to her, concern about the federal deficit is wrong. In the introduction to her book, she writes, "This book aims to drive the number of people who believe the deficit is a problem closer to zero."[2]

And there is a leftist type desire by her to knock down the rich. Aside from her theory that deficit spending is harmless, she explicitly calls for more taxes on the rich. She justifies such taxation on the grounds that it will rebalance the distribution of wealth and income. "MMT sees taxes as an important means to redress decades of stagnation and rising inequality." [3]

Kelton is currently a professor of economics and public policy at Stony Brook University and is considered a leading proponent of MMT, a theory developed by Warren Mosler.

This overview of her book will consider her theories and policy recommendations so that readers can determine the soundness of the Kelton arguments for themselves.

CHAPTER 1
JUST PRINT MONEY, MONEY, MONEY AND MORE MONEY

The short one minute elevator explanation of MMT is that it calls for the printing of money to solve all of the world's economic ills. Yup, just print the money out of thin air, taxes are not important to cover government spending but we do need government spending---a lot of it.

But, it should be pointed out that there is nothing modern about this theory.

For example, Beardsley Ruml, in 1945 during the period he was chairman of the New York Federal Reserve Bank, delivered a talk before the American Bar Association titled "Taxes for Revenue Are Obsolete." [4]

As Mises Institute president Jeff Deist notes:

> This talk, later published in *American Affairs*, makes the proto argument for MMT: sovereign national governments, with full control over their treasuries and central banks, can issue money at will to fund government expenditures. Absent any need for taxes, the justification for their continued imposition becomes social and economic, not fiscal.5

In the 1952 edition of *The Theory of Money and Credit* Ludwig von Mises commented on this theory:

> For the naive mind there is something miraculous in the issuance of fiat money. A magic word spoken by the government creates out of nothing a thing which can be exchanged against any merchandise a man would like to get. How pale is the art of sorcerers, witches, and conjurors when compared with that of the government's Treasury Department! The government, professors tell us, "can raise all the money it needs by printing it." Taxes for revenue, announced a chairman of the Federal Reserve Bank of New York, are "obsolete." How wonderful! And how malicious and misanthropic are those stubborn supporters of outdated economic orthodoxy who ask governments to balance their budgets by covering all expenditures out of tax revenue![6]

The perspective that money can be printed out of thin air is at the heart of MMT. But it is much more than just a justification for a money printing scheme. It is support for a money printing scheme embedded with many other central planning policies.

As such, there is a lot more to put under the microscope about MMT that goes well beyond the advocacy of the running of the money printing presses.

CHAPTER 2
TAXES AND THE DEVELOPMENT OF MONEY

Stephanie Kelton holds the extreme MMT view that "taxes don't actually pay for anything."[7]

Kelton, like MMT founder Warren Mosler, believes that the government spends first and then taxes or borrows.

"The government's own deficit supplies the dollars that are needed to purchase the bonds,"[8] she writes.

Their view is also that the government must have created money in the first place; otherwise there would be no demand for money. It is taxes, demanded in the form of money, that created the original demand for money, they say.

This, of course, completely ignores the possibility that money, a medium of exchange, could have emerged naturally in an economy as indirect exchange and that governments simply taxed the money that was already in circulation or could borrow money in circulation.

The prevalent thinking is that barter first took place and then indirect exchange, which resulted in the emergence of money.

But this is not how Kelton sees it. Money was created by government as a means to tax individuals and there was no evolution from barter to indirect exchange (money) in her theory.

Curiously, other than a footnote reference by Kelton pointing to claims that there wasn't much barter before indirect exchange emerged, she remarkably does not attempt to prove the essential MMT claim that taxation creates money.

But her footnote reference is stunning; it leads off by listing the book *Debt: The First 5,000 Years* by David Graeber.

Graeber is an anthropologist and makes basic economic errors in his book that no economist would ever make. He misidentifies the name of the founder of the Austrian school of economics, referring to him as Karl instead of Carl Menger.

Karl was actually the son of Carl but it was Carl who was the economist and published several books on the subject.

But more significantly, he writes that Menger, along with William Jevons, added to the idea that money developed after barter by stating that they only (emphasis added) "improved on the details of the story, **most of all by adding various mathematical equations** to demonstrate that a random assortment of people with random desires could, in theory, produce not only a single commodity to use as money but a uniform price system."[9]

But Menger never used equations in his discussion of the emergence of money, never mind as the core to his development of the theory of how barter and indirect exchange emerged. He, in fact, rejected the mathematical approach.

There are no equations used in his discussion of barter and indirect exchange at all in his books. There are no equations at all in his book *Principles of Economics*, where he discusses barter and indirect exchange or in his paper "The Origins of Money."

Graeber just gets this completely wrong.

Graeber also offers probably the best critique as to why there may be no substance to his claim that there was no barter.

In his chapter, "The Myth of Barter," he points out that the available evidence of indirect exchange early on exists because "Some of it is just the nature of the evidence: coins are preserved in archaeological record; credit arrangements are usually not."[10]

But if credit arrangements were usually not of record, just what are the chances of early stage records of barter? How and why would that be recorded?

That is, he argues there was no barter because there are no records of such but then comes pretty close to admitting that records were probably not kept at the time of barter.

On this weak Graeber reed, Kelton plows on. But do note that by her being unable to prove that money did not emerge from barter, she is creating greater technical problems for her theory down the road.

Kelton and Mosler hold the view that taxes exist to create a demand for money and this is important for them so that they can promote the idea that taxes are a necessary technical tool rather than just the taking of funds out of the private sector economy as a kind of coercion over the private sector.

If Mosler and Kelton deny money could develop in a natural manner and money only develops through government taxation, and they do deny it could occur naturally, then they have some further explaining to do.

Here is an important hurdle they can't resolve. We actually have the closest thing you are ever going to get in the social sciences to a lab experiment. Cigarettes emerged as a natural money; that is, as a medium of exchange for indirect trade, absent taxation, in German P.O.W. camps during World War 2, as reported in the fascinating 1945 paper "The Economic Organization of a P.O.W. Camp" by R.A. Radford[11].

The claim that money can only emerge via taxation is a failed claim and the Radford paper proves this.

Menger's theory, from barter to indirect exchange, however, shines even after the Radford paper. Menger wrote in the 1870s in his conclusion about the emergence of money:

> The origin of money (as distinct from coin), which is only one variety of money) is, as we have seen, entirely natural and thus displays legislative influence only in the rarest instances. Money is not an invention of the state. It is not the product of a legislative act. Even the sanction of political authority is not necessary for its existence. Certain commodities came to be money quite naturally, as a result of economic relationships that were independent of the power of the state.[12]

But Menger was a very deep, careful and thorough thinker, so he added a comment on the state adopting a money for taxes and as a general legal tender:

> But if, in response to the needs of trade, a good receives the sanction of the state as money, the result will be that not only every payment to the state itself but all other payments not explicitly contracted for in other goods can be required or offered, with legally binding effect, only in the units of that good. There will be the further, and especially important, result that one payment has originally been contracted for other goods but cannot, for some reason, be made, the payments substituted can similarly be required are offered, with legally binding effect only, in units of one particular good. Thus the sanction of the state gives a particular good the attribute of being a universal substitute in exchange, and although the state is not responsible for the existence of the money - character of the good, it is responsible for a significant improvement in its money character.[13]

Thus Menger shows that the state can become involved in the payment of exchange but this is far from arguing that the state must use the tool of taxation to create money in the first place. Indeed, Menger argued the opposite.

CHAPTER 3
PRICE INFLATION

Kelton has a schizophrenic view about price inflation measurements. On the one hand, she understands the limitations of price indexes as inflation measures:

> We can only get a general sense of what's happening to prices because it's literally impossible to track what's happening to the price of every item that's for sale in our economy.[14]

But at the same time she adopts the aggregate index measures for policymaking and ignores specific money flows that may result in price pressure in only certain sectors or even only certain goods because of money printing.

Thus, she is able to make the statement, "A deficit is only evidence of overspending if it sparks inflation."[10]

Which says nothing about specific money flows and specific sectors where price inflation may occur.

If a government is spending funds, it is bidding against others for those goods. Thus, there is a serious lack of understanding by Kelton of how government spending distorts the structure of the economy away from a private sector structure in the direction of a government structure if only aggregate price inflation measures are monitored for signs of inflation.

Kelton and the rest of the MMTers hold the odd view that demand for goods and services can at times be nonexistent and the government must thus step in.

But demand for goods and services does not disappear if the government doesn't buy them. This is a Keynesian error in thought[15]. Demand always occurs in the private sector. This is one of the major failures of MMT thinking. It does not take this structure shift into consideration. It somehow holds the view that if the government does not enter the market many prices would fall to zero. This would not occur as demonstrated by Milton Friedman in a quip some years ago.

At an international gathering of free market economists, Sir Keith Joseph, Minister of Industry in Great Britain and an alleged free market advocate in the Margaret Thatcher government, was asked why the government, despite lip service to privatization, had taken no steps to privatize the steel industry, which had been nationalized by the Labor government.

Sir Keith explained that the steel industry was losing money in government hands, and "therefore" could not command a price if put up for sale. At which point, Friedman leaped to his feet, and shouted, waving a dollar bill in the air, "I hereby bid one dollar for the British steel industry!"[16]

This goes the same for labor. I have previously stated that if labor was cheap enough ($5.00 per day), I would hire 5 servants for myself:
- A manservant who would among other things shave me every morning, get my clothes ready and put

toothpaste on my toothbrush every morning (which I understand is done for Prince Charles every morning)
- A full-time standby driver
- A full-time maid
- A jack-of-all-trades errand boy
- And, of course, a full-time cook

I am not being hyperbolic here. If labor was cheap enough, I would hire these people. But, of course, no one in the United States is going to work for me for these wages because the job alternatives they have are much better.

But it is interesting to note that when Ernest Hemingway lived in Key West and wages were low there, he had 5 servants for his family of four even though he never had guests stay at his house (They all stayed at local hotels).

I hasten to add that unemployment payments complicate this analysis but that is government intervention in the free market. Free markets clear--even labor markets. There is no need for government spending to create demand for labor; all it can do is redirect the demand away from private sector labor towards government alternatives. And, boy, is Stephanie Kelton, the interventionist, in favor of that redirection.

Since Kelton ignores the fact that markets clear, especially labor markets, she pushes for government spending to create demand for markets that she views as not clearing.

In order for her to hold this notion, it requires her to reject one of the fundamental concepts of economics: supply and demand.

In her world, there is supply that somehow isn't bought---and, thus, government needs to step in to do the buying--by deficit spending if necessary.

This is Keynesian thinking, not a "modern" theory and she knows it.

She writes:

> Outside of World War II, the US has never sustained anything approximating true full employment. The reason was spelled out in 1936 by John Maynard Keynes in his most famous book, *The General Theory of Employment, Interest, and Money*. Capitalist economies chronically operate with insufficient aggregate demand. That means there is never enough combined spending (public and private) to induce companies to offer employment for everyone who wants to work. You can come close, and you might even get there for brief periods in wartime, but peacetime economies don't operate at full capacity. There is always slack in the form of unemployed resources, including labor.[17]

It is clear that the denial of supply and demand theory is at the core of her argument. If one accepts the concept of supply and demand, involuntary unemployment cannot occur in a free market economy outside of frictional unemployment.[17]

She is making a version of the error that is known as the Lump of Labor Fallacy.

Paul Krugman explains:

Economists call it the "lump of labor fallacy." It's the idea that there is a fixed amount of work to be done in the world, so any increase in the amount each worker can produce reduces the number of available jobs.[18]

Ludwig von Mises explains what really causes *prolonged* unemployment:

> At the unhampered, market rate of wages all workers find employment...In the capitalist social order unemployment is merely a transition and friction phenomenon...
>
> The scope and duration of unemployment, interpreted today as proof of the failure of capitalism, results from the fact that labor unions and unemployment compensation are keeping wage rates higher than the unhampered market would set them. Without unemployment compensation and the power of labor unions to prevent the competition of nonmembers willing to work, the pressure of supply would soon bring about a wage adjustment that would assure employment to all hands.[19]

Yet, Kelton appears to deny this. She is hooked on government spending:

> When we run our economy below its productive capacity, it means that we are living below our collective means. The federal budget might be in deficit, but we are *underspending* whenever there is unused capacity...

When we tolerate mass unemployment, we're sacrificing whatever might have been produced...Instead of blaming Congress for failing to bring spending in line with taxes, we should accept any budget outcome that delivers broadly balanced conditions in our economy.[20]

Kelton then goes on in her book to show us just how much of a micro-technical tinkerer she is. Based on her Keynesian foundation, she wants to create a government "jobs stabilizer" program (that could involve millions of workers) for the so-called unemployed who apparently can't be helped by market adjustments in supply and demand:

> To supplement discretionary fiscal policy (the steering wheel), MMT recommends a federal job guarantee, which creates a non-discretionary automatic stabilizer that promotes both full employment and price stability.[21]

And she knows that this type of policy could result in massive money printing by the Fed.

> [T]he government simply announces a wage and then hires everyone who turns up looking for a job. If no one shows up, it means the economy is already operating at full employment. But if 15 million people show up, it reveals substantial slack. In a real sense, it's the only way to know for sure how substantially the economy is underutilizing available resources.

> Why does the financing have to come from Uncle Sam? Simple. He can't run out of money.[22]

Talk about government make-work projects. Kelton's MMT policy would be FDR government work programs on steroids:

> We're not talking about creating just any old job. This isn't a make-work scheme, aimed at simply giving the unemployed a shovel in order to justify paying them awake. It's a way to enhance the public good while strengthening our communities through a system of shared government. As [William] Vickrey put it, these public service jobs would enable us to "convert unemployed labor into improved public amenities and facilities of various types." The idea is to test people with useful work that is valued by the community and to provide compensation for that work in the form of a decent wage and benefit package.[23]

It is clear that Kelton has no appreciation for the problems with central planning, which is what these make-work programs would be.

She has no idea why Mao's China and the Soviet Union collapsed. Mao, Lenin and Stalin all called "to enhance the public good while strengthening our communities through a system of shared government" as she does.

As Mises and Nobel Prize laureate Friedrich Hayek taught us, the world is too complex at a very basic individual level for central planning to be able to succeed. There are always new inputs that can only be adjusted at a local or individual level. And then readjusted as even newer inputs emerge.

How blind of a central planner is she? She suggests setting the minimum wage at $15.00 per hour!

This would, of course, mean that no one would take a private sector job for under $15.00. Just think of how many employers of low-skilled workers, who are paid less than $15.00, wouldn't be able to find workers. This would shrink the economy and put even more people on the government make-work dole.

CHAPTER 4
HATING THE RICH

Kelton also has a typical lefty hate of the rich.

"There is a strong case to be made for taxing the rich, and we need to do it," she writes.

It is a move in the direction of pure Marxist egalitarianism. She writes:

> The purpose of the tax is not to pay for government expenditures but to help us rebalance the distribution of wealth and income because the extreme concentrations that exist today are a threat to both our democracy and to the functioning of our economy.[24]

In other words, she doesn't get how the capital which the rich supply in huge quantities drives the productivity of an economy. It is production, not redistribution that boosts the growth of an economy across the board, and Kelton doesn't seem to understand this.

She says of Amazon founder Jeff Bezos, as a justification for taxing him and the other superrich with a wealth tax, "He is more of a saver than a spender."

Precisely!

Can you imagine if Bezos, when Amazon was just an online bookstore, went and spent all his money on houses and fast cars rather than putting his money back into Amazon computers, tech workers and warehouses?

None of us would be ordering online all the things that we are able to order online now. He was the capitalist pioneer in this sector.

This is who she wants to slam a wealth tax on to limit his ability to save? One of the greatest entrepreneurs of the modern day who has a better understanding of how to deploy capital productively than nearly anyone else! This is why wealth flows to him in a free market. She has no clue.[25]

It is certainly obvious that she doesn't understand the role savings plays in financing capital investment. To her it is not about investing in capital that can produce goods and services but the investing in "financial assets" that somehow appear to her as separate from the direction of funds to the purchase of physical capital, labor and land that produces goods and services.

She writes:

> Billionaires save their wealth in the form of financial assets, real estate, fine art and rare coins.

With Kelton, there is this odd failure to connect the financing of capital that produces products. The closest she gets is her mention of "financial assets" but in context she is implying that it is merely some type of paper transaction game that doesn't help the economy when capital investment is actually the lifeblood of a growing economy.

At another point, she promotes the idea that U.S. debt is savings:

> While others refer to it as a debt clock it's really a US dollar savings clock.[27]

She is technically correct with this statement in the sense that a person who buys, say, US Treasury bills is, indeed, saving his money. But Kelton denies that such savings crowd out funds for the private sector where funds are desired to invest in real capital to produce goods and services.

She does this by assuming that most Federal debt is monetized by the Federal Reserve and, thus, she holds the incorrect view that this does not crowd out the private sector.

She writes:

> The financial crowding-out story asked us to imagine that there is a *fixed* supply of saving from which anyone can attempt to borrow...It's a straightforward supply and demand story, where the interest rate balances the demand for funding against the supply. In the absence of government deficits, all demand comes from private borrowers. There's still competition for these loanable funds, but companies are just competing with other private-sector actors for a slice of the available supply. With no competition from Uncle Sam, all savings are used to finance private investments. But, if the government's budget moves into deficit, Uncle Sam will claim some of that. As a consequence the supply of funds available to fund private investment is diminished, borrowing

costs go up, and some companies are left without financing for their projects.

MMT rejects the loanable funds story, which is rooted in the idea that borrowing is limited by access to scarce financial resources.[28]

From here she argues that the Federal Reserve can finance the government debt through printing additional dollars and thus, according to her, there is no crowding out.

But there is a great failure here in her thinking. It is not going deep enough to understand what is going on.

As we all know, there is a limited supply of resources on the planet. The entire amount of resources on the planet are bid for with money by economic actors across the land, either for consumer goods or capital goods.

If the Federal Reserve does print up new dollars to fund U.S. government deficit spending, this spending does not magically create new goods. It bids away goods from private sector actors. That is, it would bid higher than current purchasers for goods and services since that is the only way that it would be able to obtain the supply of goods and services that would otherwise be successfully bid for by private sector actors.

In other words, government debt financing via Fed monetization of U.S. debt results in the crowding out of both the private capital goods sector and the private consumer sector.

Kelton doesn't appear to understand this. She discusses crowding out only in relation to debt and interest rates, not the real economy of goods and services.

CHAPTER 5
ANTI-TRADE

Kelton is also anti-trade. She couldn't have been more clear about this in her book:

> Since 1994, when President Clinton signed NAFTA, ushering in a new era of "free trade," life has gotten steadily worse for millions of Americans. As industrial corporations have relocated their production centers to Mexico – and eventually to countries beyond North America, where they could pay workers even lower wages - millions of good-paying union jobs have disappeared. China's full accession into the World Trade Organization (WTO) in 2001 wreaked similar havoc on the US working class.[29]

An argument can certainly be made that NAFTA did not go far enough in opening up free trade; that there were too many crony side deals. But more trade is always better than less trade.

Kelton's comment on NAFTA indicates that she doesn't even understand the basic concept of comparative advantage which explains why free trade is an advantage even for those who must find new jobs because their old ones are taken over by workers in foreign lands. Her view is a pedestrian view that flies against fundamental economic thinking.

Donald J. Boudreaux writes:

When asked by mathematician Stanislaus Ulam whether he could name an idea in economics that was both universally true and not obvious, economist Paul Samuelson's example was the principle of comparative advantage.[30]

Arnold Kling writes :

On the topic of international trade, the views of economists tend to differ from those of the general public. [M]any noneconomists believe that it is more advantageous to trade with other members of one's nation or ethnic group rather than with outsiders. Economists see all forms of trade as equally advantageous.[31]

Paul Samuelson in his textbook classic, *Economics* writes:

It is not so immediately obvious, but it is no less true, that international trade is mutually profitable even when one of the two countries can produce every commodity more cheaply (in terms of all resources) than the other country... A traditional example used to illustrate this paradox of comparative advantage is the case of the best lawyer in town who is also the best typist in town. Will he not specialize in law and leave typing to the secretary? How can he afford to give up precious time from the legal field, where his comparative advantage is very great, to perform typing activities in which he has an absolute advantage but in which his relative advantage is least? Or look at it from the secretary's point of view. She is at a disadvantage relative to him at both activities; but her relative disadvantage is least in typing. Relatively speaking, she has a comparative advantage in typing.[32]

In other words, when an American worker loses a low-paying job to a foreign worker, it means the foreign worker has a comparative advantage and the American worker has the opportunity to now produce something that will be of more value to the overall economy since the foreigner has shifted the economic structure which frees up the American worker to create other things that the foreigner has a comparative disadvantage at.

Kelton's only response to this is:

> Many influential economists take the idea of comparative advantage to extremes. For instance, they argue that developing countries should focus on what they can produce most cheaply in the short term, rather than developing new industries that would enhance their monetary sovereignty over time.[33]

But notice this is not an attack on comparative advantage itself but rather an argument as to what the structure of a developing economy should look like from a central planning perspective. Rather than allowing entrepreneurs in such countries to adjust the long-term capital and short-term capital structures of the economy, she wants to central plan it.

This has nothing to do with the basic concept of comparative advantage and the observation that it makes sense to have open trade because it will be the most advantageous for raising the standard of living across the areas of trade. In other words, she never explains what she sees as the problem with comparative advantage theory itself.

As Murray Rothbard writes:

> [N]o country or region of the earth is going to be left out of the international division of labor under free trade. even if a country is in such poor shape that it has no absolute advantage in producing anything, it still pays for its trading partners, the people of other countries, to allow it to produce what it is least worst at.
>
> In this way, the citizens of every country benefit from international trade. No country is too poor or inefficient to be left out of international trade, and everyone benefits from countries specializing in what they are most best or least bad at — in other words, in whatever they have a comparative advantage.[34]

Kelton does not address this observation about international trade while at the same time attacking it.

She continues to promote the idea that for goods being produced overseas, an American worker will lose a job and will not be able to find an alternative. As I have pointed out earlier, this "no jobs" claim must by necessity deny simple supply and demand price-setting for wages.

But she is serious about believing supply and demand doesn't work for wages:

As I write this book, The International Labour Organization estimates that almost 200 million people around the world are involuntarily unemployed.[35]

Her solution?

More central planning. Once again it is about using the government to guarantee a federal job. That is structuring wages in a manner that eliminates incentives for workers to seek out free market opportunities if they are not greater than whatever the government is paying through its guarantee. This flies completely in the face of free markets.

And she wants the wage to be a "living wage;"

> MMT economists have recommended that these jobs pay a living wage and that the work itself should serve a useful public purpose. Since the job guarantee would establish a permanent commitment, it would become a mandatory (as opposed to discretionary) federal spending program.[36]

She goes on to recommend that the "living wage" be $15.00 per hour.

In other words, anyone who can't earn $15.00 in the free market economy will end up "working" for the government bureaucracy and not producing the free market goods and services that are demanded by consumers.

And, by the way, in addition to $15.00 per hour, these government employees would get health benefits and paid leave.

This is nothing but a call to distort the economic structure in the direction of central planning where free market exchange is replaced by what Mises called the Führer Principle. That is the leader, or leaders, of a government make decisions about worker deployment and what is produced.

Does this central planning really need to occur, if there is no problem in the first place for workers to find jobs in the free market, jobs that are in demand to produce goods and services that consumers desire?

Kelton is advocating a bad policy fix, central planning, for a problem that doesn't exist.

CHAPTER 6
DEFICITS DON'T MATTER

Of course, all these Kelton-proposed programs cost money but she does not see that as a problem.

From her point of view, deficits are not a problem. When the government spends more than it is taking in, the Federal Reserve should just print the money.

There are a number of problems with this view.

First, such money printing distorts the structure of the economy. As I have pointed out above, new money introduced in the economy results in goods and services of the economic actors with the new money being able to bid goods and services away from some who would have been successful bidders without the money created and provided to the winning Fed new money holding bidders.

In a very real sense, this is price inflation that is faced immediately by the losing bidders created by the money printing environment.

Kelton does not appear to see this, and she certainly doesn't discuss it.

For her, price inflation doesn't appear to be a problem until it reveals itself in government price indexes. And most interestingly, nowhere in the book does Kelton provide a number as to how high price inflation would have to advance before she would see it as a concern.

One gets the sense from the book that Kelton's price inflation danger point is something like that of an alcoholic who will fix his drinking problem tomorrow or the day after but certainly not today.

"Too little, not too much, inflation has plagued the US, Japan and Europe," she writes.

MMTers in general are really not that much concerned about price inflation.

Here is an email exchange I had in April 2019 with another top MMTer, Randal Wray:

> **Wenzel email:**
> Subject: Inflation question
> Dear Prof. Wray,
> In your response to Doug Henwood, I note that you write:
>
> "If there were a prolonged stretch of inflation we would—of course—recommend proactively raising taxes and/or reducing spending."
>
> What inflation rate would you consider high enough that proactively raising taxes and/or reducing spending should be implemented? And is there a particular length of time that should be linked to such a rate of inflation before a call for the proactive measures?

Thank you for your help on this matter.

Best regards,

Robert Wenzel
Editor & Publisher
EconomicPolicyJournal.com
San Francisco, CA

Wray's response:

I do not think one number fits all cases. Depends on whether the rising prices are broad-based (across the components of the CPI)--if so, I'd recommend after a relatively short period of time--four years?--and sooner if it was accelerating. If it was across a few categories (which has always been the case in the USA since the late 1960s) I'd probably wait longer to see what happens (and take other approaches to fighting the pressures instead). You want to try to determine if the cause is excessive aggregate demand (then raising taxes could be appropriate) or if it comes on the supply side (in which case raising taxes is a poor choice).

L. Randall Wray
Senior Scholar, Levy Economics Institute
Professor of Economics, Bard College

Wenzel email:

Thank you for your prompt reply.

If it is a case of broad-based inflation crossing the Fed's target of 2%, say to 2.5%, would that be the type of inflation you might act on after 4 or more years? Or would it be inflation at 3% or 5% that would concern you?

Thank you once again for your help on this matter.

Wray email:

not 2 or 2.5%. at a level that low you cannot tell if there is even inflation. could be measurement error. if it was sustained above 4 you'd be pretty sure there was actually inflation pressure (especially if broad based)

So it appears that Wray would only be concerned with price inflation of 3% or 5% if it lasted for 4 or more years!

I then emailed the founder of MMT, Warren Mosler, for his take:

Wenzel email:

Dear Mr. Mosler,
I recently had the below email exchange with Prof. Wray.

A Top MMTer Informs: When Exactly MMTers Would Start to Battle Price Inflation$_{GG}$

I am wondering if your thinking on rates of inflation and length of inflation that would be a concern is in line with his.

Thank you for your help on this matter.

Robert Wenzel
EconomicPolicyJournal.com

Mosler email response:

That's entirely a political decision.

Inflation doesn't hurt output and employment, and may even help, according to studies.

But generally voters don't like it.

So politicians respond to the voters in that regard.

Best

Warren

Is there any wonder why voters don't like it? It cuts into their buying power and benefits those the Fed gives the money to first. Also, note well, Mosler does not mention at all the fact that Fed money printing must, out of the gate, distort the structure of the economy. He is implying what Kelton promotes in her book; that supply and demand in a free market doesn't clear for some reason.

But let us assume that at some point price inflation is high enough that it concerns Kelton, Mosler and Wray. One of their solutions is to increase taxes. But increasing taxes just distorts the economy further unless the taxes are the exact money that was pumped into the economy by the Federal Reserve in the first place and those taxed are the ones who first received it.

That is not going to happen.

The MMT tax proposal is making a class of taxpayers pay for a price inflation that benefited a different group.

How does this make any sense?

But the big question that must be asked is why distort in the first place with the money pump and then distort from another direction with taxes?

This is all about a central planning scheme that just isn't necessary if you understand the basic theory of supply and demand that markets clear.

Indeed, even the business cycles that so concern Keynesians are about central bank money pump distortions in the first place.[37]

CONCLUSION

Kelton's advocacy for government spending is just another dressed up Keynesian justification for the money pump---with a more aggressive money pump and more aggressive central planning schemes.

It is difficult to understand how anyone steeped in economic history and economic theory would walk away from the reading of this book with other than absolute horror.

It is confusion about economics on a very basic level that leads to even more complex confusion at the policy recommendation level.

The notion that government deficits, regardless of the way they are financed, do not result in an immediate distortion of the economy is simply not true.

Deficit spending moves the economy away from free market activity and expands bureaucratic state activity that is at the heart of central planning.

In a complex world with billions of changing inputs, central planning can never adjust to economic conditions the way free markets can.

Failure to recognize this is the serious problem with Modern Monetary Theory. It goes beyond just aggressive money printing, which is a serious problem in itself, but it is a failure to grasp the problems of central planning involved in the policy recommendations that emerge from MMT.

If you come across anyone touting MMT, they do not understand any of this. And there are many at present touting it and that is a big problem.

Endnotes

1. https://epj.cloud/manjoo
2. Stephanie Kelton, *The Deficit Myth: Modern Monetary Theory and the Birth of the People's Economy* (Public Affairs, 2020) p. 8
3. Ibid, p. 34
4. https://epj.cloud/ruml
5. https://epj.cloud/Deist
6. Ludwig von Mises, *The Theory of Money and Credit* (Johnathan Cape Limited, 1952) p.418
7. Kelton, p. 23
8. Ibid. p. 106
9. David Graeber, *Debt: The First 5,000 Years* (Melville House, 2014) p. 28
10. Ibid, p. 22-23
11. https://epj.cloud/radford
12. Carl Menger, *Principles of Economics* (Ludwig Von Mises Institute, 2007) p. 261
13. Menger, op. cit.
14. Kelton, p. 14
15. Henry Hazlitt, *The Failure of the "New Economics"* (Ludwig Von Mises Institute, 2011) pp. 32-43
16. https://epj.cloud/bid
17. Kelton, p. 56
18. https://epj.cloud/lumpoflabor
19. Mises, *A Critique of Interventionism* (Foundation for Economic Education, 1996) p.15
20. Kelton, p. 60
21. Ibid., p.64
22. Ibid
23. Ibid, p.67

24. Ibid.
25. I hasten to add that I am referencing here the free market entrepreneurial work that Bezos does and not the crony deals he does with governments.
26. Kelton, op. cit.
27. Ibid, p. 69
28. Ibid, p. 113
29. Ibid, p. 129
30. https://epj.cloud/CA
31. https://epj.cloud/kling
32. Paul Samuelson, *Economics: The Original 1948 Edition* (McGraw Hill Education, 1997) p.540
33. Kelton, p. 150
34. Murray Rothbard, *Classical Economics: An Austrian Perspective on the History of Economic Thought* (Ludwig Von Mises Institute, 2006) P. 95
35. Kelton, p. 152
36. Ibid, p. 246
37. Murray Rothbard, *Austrian School Business Cycle Theory* (Gallatin House, 2014)

Robert Wenzel is editor & publisher of EconomicPolicyJournal.com

He can be reached at rw@epjmail.com

He resides in San Francisco.

Made in the USA
Las Vegas, NV
24 March 2021